Timed Math

DIVISION

REM 504

A TEACHING RESOURCE FROM

REMEDIA
PUBLICATIONS

To find Remedia products in a store near you, visit:
www.rempub.com/stores

REMEDIA PUBLICATIONS, INC.
15887 N. 76TH STREET • SUITE 120 • SCOTTSDALE, AZ • 85260

RESEARCH-BASED ACTIVITIES
Supports State & National Standards

This product utilizes innovative strategies and proven methods to improve student learning. The product is based upon reliable research and effective practices that have been replicated in classrooms across the United States. Information regarding the research basis is provided on our website at www.rempub.com/research

1

INTRODUCTION

Timed Math Drills - Division provides step-by-step drills in division that start with wholepage calculations using the same, single divisor (1 through 9); progress to calculations using two different divisors, and then to all-inclusive, mixed divisors.

The goal is to achieve mastery at the highest possible accuracy level in the lowest possible time. Determine th time given to complete the drills based on students' ability levels. A chart is included on which each student's progress can be recorded. For those students who exhibit low accuracy scores or slow completion, repeated attempts at working the troublesome pages is recommended. Those students who do quite well initially might enjoy the challenge of repeating the drills in order to achieve "personal best" times. Award certificates are included to validate students' achievements.

CONTENTS

Name _____

Time _____

Number Correct _____ / 100

Division Facts • ÷ 1's

$1\overline{)2}$ $1\overline{)3}$ $1\overline{)6}$ $1\overline{)0}$ $1\overline{)9}$ $1\overline{)4}$ $1\overline{)7}$ $1\overline{)3}$ $1\overline{)5}$ $1\overline{)1}$

$1\overline{)5}$ $1\overline{)4}$ $1\overline{)8}$ $1\overline{)3}$ $1\overline{)6}$ $1\overline{)1}$ $1\overline{)2}$ $1\overline{)7}$ $1\overline{)9}$ $1\overline{)0}$

$1\overline{)0}$ $1\overline{)2}$ $1\overline{)9}$ $1\overline{)7}$ $1\overline{)4}$ $1\overline{)8}$ $1\overline{)1}$ $1\overline{)3}$ $1\overline{)5}$ $1\overline{)6}$

$1\overline{)9}$ $1\overline{)5}$ $1\overline{)4}$ $1\overline{)8}$ $1\overline{)0}$ $1\overline{)6}$ $1\overline{)3}$ $1\overline{)2}$ $1\overline{)7}$ $1\overline{)1}$

$1\overline{)2}$ $1\overline{)6}$ $1\overline{)3}$ $1\overline{)1}$ $1\overline{)9}$ $1\overline{)7}$ $1\overline{)4}$ $1\overline{)0}$ $1\overline{)8}$ $1\overline{)5}$

$1\overline{)7}$ $1\overline{)9}$ $1\overline{)0}$ $1\overline{)5}$ $1\overline{)3}$ $1\overline{)8}$ $1\overline{)2}$ $1\overline{)6}$ $1\overline{)1}$ $1\overline{)4}$

$1\overline{)6}$ $1\overline{)2}$ $1\overline{)4}$ $1\overline{)8}$ $1\overline{)1}$ $1\overline{)0}$ $1\overline{)7}$ $1\overline{)3}$ $1\overline{)5}$ $1\overline{)9}$

$1\overline{)6}$ $1\overline{)8}$ $1\overline{)9}$ $1\overline{)2}$ $1\overline{)7}$ $1\overline{)9}$ $1\overline{)4}$ $1\overline{)5}$ $1\overline{)8}$ $1\overline{)0}$

$1\overline{)4}$ $1\overline{)3}$ $1\overline{)8}$ $1\overline{)5}$ $1\overline{)6}$ $1\overline{)3}$ $1\overline{)2}$ $1\overline{)6}$ $1\overline{)1}$ $1\overline{)4}$

$1\overline{)2}$ $1\overline{)0}$ $1\overline{)7}$ $1\overline{)3}$ $1\overline{)1}$ $1\overline{)7}$ $1\overline{)0}$ $1\overline{)9}$ $1\overline{)5}$ $1\overline{)3}$

Name _____

Time _____

Number Correct _____ / 100

Division Facts • ÷ 2's

2⟌2	2⟌6	2⟌12	2⟌0	2⟌18	2⟌16	2⟌4	2⟌12	2⟌2	2⟌8
2⟌10	2⟌4	2⟌8	2⟌6	2⟌12	2⟌4	2⟌6	2⟌10	2⟌0	2⟌12
2⟌0	2⟌2	2⟌18	2⟌14	2⟌8	2⟌2	2⟌4	2⟌14	2⟌18	2⟌0
2⟌18	2⟌10	2⟌8	2⟌16	2⟌0	2⟌4	2⟌6	2⟌16	2⟌10	2⟌4
2⟌4	2⟌12	2⟌6	2⟌2	2⟌18	2⟌12	2⟌18	2⟌4	2⟌14	2⟌2
2⟌14	2⟌18	2⟌0	2⟌10	2⟌6	2⟌14	2⟌8	2⟌0	2⟌16	2⟌10
2⟌12	2⟌4	2⟌8	2⟌2	2⟌0	2⟌16	2⟌4	2⟌12	2⟌2	2⟌8
2⟌8	2⟌18	2⟌2	2⟌14	2⟌12	2⟌18	2⟌8	2⟌10	2⟌16	2⟌0
2⟌10	2⟌6	2⟌16	2⟌10	2⟌6	2⟌16	2⟌4	2⟌12	2⟌2	2⟌8
2⟌0	2⟌14	2⟌6	2⟌18	2⟌12	2⟌14	2⟌0	2⟌18	2⟌10	2⟌6

Name _____

Division Facts • ÷ 3's

$3\overline{)6}$ $3\overline{)9}$ $3\overline{)18}$ $3\overline{)27}$ $3\overline{)0}$ $3\overline{)9}$ $3\overline{)12}$ $3\overline{)21}$ $3\overline{)15}$ $3\overline{)18}$

$3\overline{)15}$ $3\overline{)12}$ $3\overline{)24}$ $3\overline{)9}$ $3\overline{)12}$ $3\overline{)18}$ $3\overline{)21}$ $3\overline{)6}$ $3\overline{)0}$ $3\overline{)12}$

$3\overline{)0}$ $3\overline{)6}$ $3\overline{)27}$ $3\overline{)24}$ $3\overline{)9}$ $3\overline{)21}$ $3\overline{)3}$ $3\overline{)9}$ $3\overline{)18}$ $3\overline{)15}$

$3\overline{)27}$ $3\overline{)15}$ $3\overline{)12}$ $3\overline{)24}$ $3\overline{)0}$ $3\overline{)18}$ $3\overline{)9}$ $3\overline{)6}$ $3\overline{)21}$ $3\overline{)3}$

$3\overline{)6}$ $3\overline{)24}$ $3\overline{)9}$ $3\overline{)3}$ $3\overline{)27}$ $3\overline{)21}$ $3\overline{)12}$ $3\overline{)0}$ $3\overline{)24}$ $3\overline{)15}$

$3\overline{)21}$ $3\overline{)27}$ $3\overline{)0}$ $3\overline{)15}$ $3\overline{)9}$ $3\overline{)24}$ $3\overline{)6}$ $3\overline{)18}$ $3\overline{)3}$ $3\overline{)12}$

$3\overline{)12}$ $3\overline{)6}$ $3\overline{)18}$ $3\overline{)3}$ $3\overline{)24}$ $3\overline{)0}$ $3\overline{)21}$ $3\overline{)9}$ $3\overline{)15}$ $3\overline{)27}$

$3\overline{)24}$ $3\overline{)27}$ $3\overline{)6}$ $3\overline{)21}$ $3\overline{)6}$ $3\overline{)27}$ $3\overline{)12}$ $3\overline{)15}$ $3\overline{)24}$ $3\overline{)0}$

$3\overline{)9}$ $3\overline{)24}$ $3\overline{)12}$ $3\overline{)24}$ $3\overline{)18}$ $3\overline{)9}$ $3\overline{)27}$ $3\overline{)18}$ $3\overline{)3}$ $3\overline{)12}$

$3\overline{)6}$ $3\overline{)0}$ $3\overline{)21}$ $3\overline{)9}$ $3\overline{)3}$ $3\overline{)21}$ $3\overline{)0}$ $3\overline{)27}$ $3\overline{)15}$ $3\overline{)9}$

   Timed Math Drills - Division

Name _____

Time _____

Number Correct _____ / 100

Division Facts • ÷ 4's

4⟌8	4⟌12	4⟌0	4⟌36	4⟌12	4⟌24	4⟌16	4⟌28	4⟌20	4⟌4
4⟌20	4⟌16	4⟌32	4⟌12	4⟌24	4⟌4	4⟌8	4⟌36	4⟌0	4⟌16
4⟌0	4⟌8	4⟌36	4⟌28	4⟌16	4⟌32	4⟌4	4⟌12	4⟌20	4⟌24
4⟌36	4⟌20	4⟌16	4⟌32	4⟌0	4⟌24	4⟌12	4⟌8	4⟌28	4⟌4
4⟌8	4⟌16	4⟌12	4⟌4	4⟌32	4⟌28	4⟌16	4⟌0	4⟌36	4⟌20
4⟌28	4⟌36	4⟌0	4⟌20	4⟌12	4⟌32	4⟌8	4⟌24	4⟌4	4⟌16
4⟌24	4⟌8	4⟌16	4⟌28	4⟌36	4⟌4	4⟌0	4⟌32	4⟌12	4⟌20
4⟌24	4⟌12	4⟌36	4⟌8	4⟌28	4⟌36	4⟌16	4⟌20	4⟌32	4⟌0
4⟌12	4⟌32	4⟌20	4⟌24	4⟌4	4⟌12	4⟌8	4⟌16	4⟌24	4⟌4
4⟌8	4⟌0	4⟌28	4⟌12	4⟌8	4⟌28	4⟌0	4⟌36	4⟌20	4⟌12

Division Facts • ÷ 5's

5⟌10	5⟌15	5⟌30	5⟌0	5⟌45	5⟌15	5⟌20	5⟌35	5⟌25	5⟌5
5⟌25	5⟌20	5⟌45	5⟌15	5⟌20	5⟌5	5⟌10	5⟌40	5⟌35	5⟌30
5⟌0	5⟌10	5⟌45	5⟌35	5⟌20	5⟌40	5⟌5	5⟌10	5⟌25	5⟌40
5⟌45	5⟌25	5⟌20	5⟌40	5⟌0	5⟌30	5⟌10	5⟌15	5⟌30	5⟌5
5⟌10	5⟌30	5⟌15	5⟌5	5⟌45	5⟌35	5⟌20	5⟌0	5⟌40	5⟌25
5⟌35	5⟌45	5⟌0	5⟌25	5⟌15	5⟌40	5⟌10	5⟌30	5⟌5	5⟌20
5⟌30	5⟌10	5⟌20	5⟌40	5⟌5	5⟌0	5⟌30	5⟌15	5⟌25	5⟌45
5⟌30	5⟌40	5⟌45	5⟌10	5⟌35	5⟌45	5⟌20	5⟌5	5⟌35	5⟌0
5⟌40	5⟌0	5⟌25	5⟌5	5⟌45	5⟌15	5⟌10	5⟌30	5⟌5	5⟌20
5⟌10	5⟌35	5⟌5	5⟌0	5⟌30	5⟌35	5⟌0	5⟌45	5⟌25	5⟌15

Name _____

Time _____

Number Correct _____ / 100

Division Facts • ÷ 6's

$6\overline{)12}$ $6\overline{)18}$ $6\overline{)36}$ $6\overline{)0}$ $6\overline{)54}$ $6\overline{)18}$ $6\overline{)24}$ $6\overline{)42}$ $6\overline{)30}$ $6\overline{)6}$

$6\overline{)30}$ $6\overline{)24}$ $6\overline{)18}$ $6\overline{)36}$ $6\overline{)42}$ $6\overline{)6}$ $6\overline{)12}$ $6\overline{)48}$ $6\overline{)54}$ $6\overline{)0}$

$6\overline{)0}$ $6\overline{)12}$ $6\overline{)54}$ $6\overline{)42}$ $6\overline{)24}$ $6\overline{)48}$ $6\overline{)6}$ $6\overline{)18}$ $6\overline{)30}$ $6\overline{)36}$

$6\overline{)54}$ $6\overline{)30}$ $6\overline{)24}$ $6\overline{)48}$ $6\overline{)0}$ $6\overline{)36}$ $6\overline{)18}$ $6\overline{)12}$ $6\overline{)42}$ $6\overline{)6}$

$6\overline{)12}$ $6\overline{)36}$ $6\overline{)18}$ $6\overline{)6}$ $6\overline{)54}$ $6\overline{)42}$ $6\overline{)24}$ $6\overline{)0}$ $6\overline{)48}$ $6\overline{)30}$

$6\overline{)42}$ $6\overline{)54}$ $6\overline{)0}$ $6\overline{)30}$ $6\overline{)18}$ $6\overline{)48}$ $6\overline{)12}$ $6\overline{)36}$ $6\overline{)6}$ $6\overline{)24}$

$6\overline{)30}$ $6\overline{)12}$ $6\overline{)24}$ $6\overline{)48}$ $6\overline{)6}$ $6\overline{)0}$ $6\overline{)42}$ $6\overline{)18}$ $6\overline{)30}$ $6\overline{)54}$

$6\overline{)36}$ $6\overline{)48}$ $6\overline{)54}$ $6\overline{)12}$ $6\overline{)42}$ $6\overline{)54}$ $6\overline{)24}$ $6\overline{)30}$ $6\overline{)48}$ $6\overline{)0}$

$6\overline{)24}$ $6\overline{)18}$ $6\overline{)48}$ $6\overline{)30}$ $6\overline{)36}$ $6\overline{)18}$ $6\overline{)12}$ $6\overline{)36}$ $6\overline{)6}$ $6\overline{)24}$

$6\overline{)12}$ $6\overline{)0}$ $6\overline{)42}$ $6\overline{)18}$ $6\overline{)6}$ $6\overline{)0}$ $6\overline{)54}$ $6\overline{)30}$ $6\overline{)18}$ $6\overline{)42}$

Division Facts • ÷ 7's

7$\overline{)28}$	7$\overline{)56}$	7$\overline{)63}$	7$\overline{)42}$	7$\overline{)7}$	7$\overline{)28}$	7$\overline{)49}$	7$\overline{)0}$	7$\overline{)63}$	7$\overline{)35}$
7$\overline{)14}$	7$\overline{)0}$	7$\overline{)49}$	7$\overline{)21}$	7$\overline{)14}$	7$\overline{)49}$	7$\overline{)0}$	7$\overline{)63}$	7$\overline{)56}$	7$\overline{)21}$
7$\overline{)7}$	7$\overline{)28}$	7$\overline{)14}$	7$\overline{)35}$	7$\overline{)7}$	7$\overline{)14}$	7$\overline{)21}$	7$\overline{)42}$	7$\overline{)0}$	7$\overline{)63}$
7$\overline{)0}$	7$\overline{)14}$	7$\overline{)49}$	7$\overline{)63}$	7$\overline{)0}$	7$\overline{)56}$	7$\overline{)28}$	7$\overline{)56}$	7$\overline{)21}$	7$\overline{)42}$
7$\overline{)56}$	7$\overline{)7}$	7$\overline{)28}$	7$\overline{)35}$	7$\overline{)42}$	7$\overline{)0}$	7$\overline{)14}$	7$\overline{)28}$	7$\overline{)49}$	7$\overline{)28}$
7$\overline{)42}$	7$\overline{)28}$	7$\overline{)21}$	7$\overline{)49}$	7$\overline{)7}$	7$\overline{)63}$	7$\overline{)35}$	7$\overline{)63}$	7$\overline{)56}$	7$\overline{)0}$
7$\overline{)49}$	7$\overline{)21}$	7$\overline{)0}$	7$\overline{)56}$	7$\overline{)42}$	7$\overline{)14}$	7$\overline{)42}$	7$\overline{)28}$	7$\overline{)7}$	7$\overline{)63}$
7$\overline{)56}$	7$\overline{)14}$	7$\overline{)42}$	7$\overline{)7}$	7$\overline{)28}$	7$\overline{)49}$	7$\overline{)63}$	7$\overline{)0}$	7$\overline{)35}$	7$\overline{)21}$
7$\overline{)0}$	7$\overline{)49}$	7$\overline{)21}$	7$\overline{)35}$	7$\overline{)63}$	7$\overline{)42}$	7$\overline{)14}$	7$\overline{)28}$	7$\overline{)56}$	7$\overline{)7}$
7$\overline{)63}$	7$\overline{)28}$	7$\overline{)35}$	7$\overline{)56}$	7$\overline{)0}$	7$\overline{)7}$	7$\overline{)56}$	7$\overline{)63}$	7$\overline{)14}$	7$\overline{)49}$

Division Facts • ÷ 8's

8)16	8)24	8)48	8)0	8)72	8)24	8)32	8)56	8)40	8)8
8)40	8)48	8)64	8)16	8)32	8)8	8)16	8)56	8)72	8)0
8)0	8)16	8)72	8)56	8)32	8)64	8)8	8)24	8)40	8)48
8)72	8)32	8)40	8)64	8)0	8)48	8)24	8)16	8)56	8)8
8)16	8)48	8)24	8)8	8)72	8)56	8)32	8)0	8)64	8)40
8)56	8)72	8)0	8)40	8)24	8)64	8)16	8)48	8)8	8)32
8)48	8)16	8)32	8)64	8)8	8)0	8)56	8)24	8)40	8)72
8)48	8)64	8)72	8)16	8)56	8)72	8)32	8)40	8)64	8)0
8)32	8)64	8)40	8)48	8)0	8)24	8)16	8)48	8)8	8)32
8)24	8)0	8)16	8)56	8)8	8)56	8)0	8)72	8)40	8)24

Name _____   Time _____

Number Correct _____ / 100

Division Facts • ÷ 9's

$9\overline{)18}$ $9\overline{)27}$ $9\overline{)54}$ $9\overline{)0}$ $9\overline{)81}$ $9\overline{)27}$ $9\overline{)36}$ $9\overline{)63}$ $9\overline{)45}$ $9\overline{)9}$

$9\overline{)45}$ $9\overline{)63}$ $9\overline{)72}$ $9\overline{)27}$ $9\overline{)54}$ $9\overline{)9}$ $9\overline{)18}$ $9\overline{)72}$ $9\overline{)81}$ $9\overline{)9}$

$9\overline{)0}$ $9\overline{)18}$ $9\overline{)81}$ $9\overline{)63}$ $9\overline{)36}$ $9\overline{)72}$ $9\overline{)9}$ $9\overline{)27}$ $9\overline{)45}$ $9\overline{)54}$

$9\overline{)81}$ $9\overline{)27}$ $9\overline{)36}$ $9\overline{)45}$ $9\overline{)72}$ $9\overline{)0}$ $9\overline{)54}$ $9\overline{)27}$ $9\overline{)18}$ $9\overline{)27}$

$9\overline{)18}$ $9\overline{)54}$ $9\overline{)27}$ $9\overline{)9}$ $9\overline{)81}$ $9\overline{)63}$ $9\overline{)81}$ $9\overline{)0}$ $9\overline{)72}$ $9\overline{)45}$

$9\overline{)63}$ $9\overline{)81}$ $9\overline{)0}$ $9\overline{)45}$ $9\overline{)27}$ $9\overline{)72}$ $9\overline{)18}$ $9\overline{)54}$ $9\overline{)9}$ $9\overline{)36}$

$9\overline{)54}$ $9\overline{)18}$ $9\overline{)36}$ $9\overline{)72}$ $9\overline{)9}$ $9\overline{)0}$ $9\overline{)63}$ $9\overline{)27}$ $9\overline{)45}$ $9\overline{)81}$

$9\overline{)54}$ $9\overline{)72}$ $9\overline{)81}$ $9\overline{)18}$ $9\overline{)63}$ $9\overline{)0}$ $9\overline{)63}$ $9\overline{)9}$ $9\overline{)18}$ $9\overline{)0}$

$9\overline{)36}$ $9\overline{)72}$ $9\overline{)45}$ $9\overline{)27}$ $9\overline{)54}$ $9\overline{)27}$ $9\overline{)54}$ $9\overline{)18}$ $9\overline{)9}$ $9\overline{)36}$

$9\overline{)18}$ $9\overline{)27}$ $9\overline{)0}$ $9\overline{)63}$ $9\overline{)9}$ $9\overline{)63}$ $9\overline{)0}$ $9\overline{)81}$ $9\overline{)45}$ $9\overline{)27}$

Division Facts • ÷ 1's and 2's

$1\overline{)0}$ $1\overline{)2}$ $2\overline{)18}$ $1\overline{)4}$ $1\overline{)7}$ $2\overline{)12}$ $1\overline{)1}$ $1\overline{)9}$ $2\overline{)8}$ $2\overline{)16}$

$1\overline{)2}$ $2\overline{)0}$ $2\overline{)4}$ $1\overline{)3}$ $1\overline{)5}$ $2\overline{)6}$ $2\overline{)10}$ $1\overline{)6}$ $1\overline{)8}$ $2\overline{)14}$

$2\overline{)4}$ $2\overline{)18}$ $1\overline{)4}$ $1\overline{)2}$ $2\overline{)10}$ $1\overline{)6}$ $2\overline{)14}$ $2\overline{)6}$ $1\overline{)2}$ $1\overline{)1}$

$2\overline{)16}$ $2\overline{)8}$ $1\overline{)9}$ $1\overline{)0}$ $2\overline{)4}$ $2\overline{)12}$ $1\overline{)7}$ $2\overline{)10}$ $1\overline{)3}$ $2\overline{)14}$

$2\overline{)6}$ $1\overline{)4}$ $2\overline{)16}$ $1\overline{)6}$ $1\overline{)3}$ $2\overline{)18}$ $2\overline{)8}$ $1\overline{)6}$ $2\overline{)10}$ $1\overline{)7}$

$2\overline{)14}$ $2\overline{)8}$ $1\overline{)2}$ $1\overline{)0}$ $2\overline{)18}$ $1\overline{)8}$ $2\overline{)14}$ $1\overline{)4}$ $1\overline{)5}$ $2\overline{)12}$

$1\overline{)1}$ $2\overline{)4}$ $1\overline{)5}$ $2\overline{)0}$ $2\overline{)10}$ $1\overline{)7}$ $2\overline{)12}$ $1\overline{)5}$ $2\overline{)18}$ $1\overline{)6}$

$2\overline{)18}$ $1\overline{)8}$ $2\overline{)14}$ $2\overline{)16}$ $1\overline{)9}$ $2\overline{)12}$ $1\overline{)4}$ $2\overline{)6}$ $1\overline{)0}$ $2\overline{)0}$

$2\overline{)10}$ $1\overline{)3}$ $2\overline{)4}$ $1\overline{)4}$ $2\overline{)10}$ $1\overline{)6}$ $2\overline{)16}$ $1\overline{)5}$ $1\overline{)6}$ $2\overline{)6}$

$2\overline{)6}$ $2\overline{)8}$ $2\overline{)0}$ $2\overline{)4}$ $1\overline{)9}$ $1\overline{)8}$ $2\overline{)14}$ $2\overline{)8}$ $1\overline{)5}$ $2\overline{)12}$

Division Facts • ÷ 2's and 3's

$2\overline{)4}$	$3\overline{)0}$	$3\overline{)27}$	$2\overline{)8}$	$2\overline{)0}$	$3\overline{)21}$	$2\overline{)6}$	$3\overline{)24}$	$2\overline{)12}$	$3\overline{)12}$
$2\overline{)6}$	$2\overline{)2}$	$3\overline{)3}$	$3\overline{)18}$	$2\overline{)10}$	$2\overline{)18}$	$3\overline{)15}$	$2\overline{)14}$	$3\overline{)9}$	$3\overline{)6}$
$3\overline{)27}$	$2\overline{)10}$	$2\overline{)4}$	$3\overline{)6}$	$3\overline{)18}$	$2\overline{)6}$	$2\overline{)12}$	$3\overline{)15}$	$3\overline{)24}$	$2\overline{)14}$
$2\overline{)10}$	$3\overline{)21}$	$3\overline{)15}$	$2\overline{)8}$	$2\overline{)4}$	$2\overline{)0}$	$2\overline{)2}$	$3\overline{)21}$	$2\overline{)12}$	$3\overline{)12}$
$3\overline{)18}$	$2\overline{)6}$	$3\overline{)12}$	$2\overline{)12}$	$3\overline{)9}$	$2\overline{)10}$	$3\overline{)24}$	$2\overline{)14}$	$3\overline{)9}$	$2\overline{)4}$
$3\overline{)24}$	$2\overline{)18}$	$2\overline{)0}$	$3\overline{)18}$	$2\overline{)14}$	$3\overline{)27}$	$3\overline{)12}$	$2\overline{)4}$	$2\overline{)10}$	$3\overline{)12}$
$3\overline{)12}$	$2\overline{)4}$	$3\overline{)18}$	$3\overline{)15}$	$2\overline{)8}$	$2\overline{)4}$	$2\overline{)2}$	$2\overline{)6}$	$2\overline{)12}$	$2\overline{)18}$
$3\overline{)9}$	$3\overline{)0}$	$2\overline{)8}$	$3\overline{)27}$	$3\overline{)3}$	$2\overline{)2}$	$2\overline{)0}$	$3\overline{)24}$	$3\overline{)18}$	$2\overline{)16}$
$3\overline{)15}$	$2\overline{)8}$	$3\overline{)24}$	$2\overline{)14}$	$3\overline{)18}$	$3\overline{)27}$	$2\overline{)0}$	$3\overline{)3}$	$3\overline{)12}$	$2\overline{)4}$
$2\overline{)18}$	$3\overline{)12}$	$3\overline{)6}$	$2\overline{)18}$	$2\overline{)12}$	$3\overline{)24}$	$3\overline{)21}$	$3\overline{)15}$	$2\overline{)12}$	$3\overline{)21}$

Name _____

Division Facts • ÷ 3's and 4's

$3\overline{)27}$ $4\overline{)0}$ $3\overline{)3}$ $4\overline{)4}$ $3\overline{)9}$ $4\overline{)20}$ $3\overline{)12}$ $3\overline{)0}$ $4\overline{)8}$ $4\overline{)32}$

$3\overline{)15}$ $4\overline{)12}$ $3\overline{)6}$ $3\overline{)18}$ $4\overline{)28}$ $3\overline{)21}$ $4\overline{)24}$ $4\overline{)16}$ $3\overline{)24}$ $4\overline{)36}$

$4\overline{)32}$ $4\overline{)0}$ $3\overline{)0}$ $3\overline{)6}$ $4\overline{)4}$ $3\overline{)9}$ $4\overline{)20}$ $4\overline{)4}$ $3\overline{)18}$ $4\overline{)28}$

$3\overline{)9}$ $3\overline{)27}$ $4\overline{)4}$ $4\overline{)32}$ $4\overline{)0}$ $3\overline{)6}$ $4\overline{)36}$ $4\overline{)32}$ $4\overline{)16}$ $3\overline{)18}$

$4\overline{)32}$ $4\overline{)8}$ $3\overline{)15}$ $4\overline{)12}$ $3\overline{)0}$ $3\overline{)12}$ $3\overline{)6}$ $3\overline{)18}$ $4\overline{)20}$ $3\overline{)9}$

$4\overline{)28}$ $4\overline{)4}$ $4\overline{)24}$ $3\overline{)3}$ $4\overline{)16}$ $4\overline{)0}$ $3\overline{)24}$ $3\overline{)27}$ $4\overline{)36}$ $3\overline{)21}$

$4\overline{)4}$ $4\overline{)32}$ $3\overline{)15}$ $4\overline{)16}$ $3\overline{)3}$ $4\overline{)28}$ $3\overline{)0}$ $3\overline{)6}$ $4\overline{)36}$ $3\overline{)12}$

$4\overline{)20}$ $4\overline{)0}$ $4\overline{)24}$ $3\overline{)9}$ $3\overline{)24}$ $3\overline{)9}$ $4\overline{)16}$ $4\overline{)4}$ $3\overline{)0}$ $3\overline{)27}$

$4\overline{)12}$ $4\overline{)36}$ $3\overline{)6}$ $3\overline{)27}$ $3\overline{)18}$ $3\overline{)15}$ $4\overline{)0}$ $3\overline{)3}$ $4\overline{)16}$ $4\overline{)24}$

$3\overline{)18}$ $3\overline{)9}$ $4\overline{)0}$ $3\overline{)3}$ $4\overline{)20}$ $3\overline{)18}$ $4\overline{)16}$ $4\overline{)4}$ $3\overline{)21}$ $4\overline{)32}$

Name _____

Time _____

Number Correct _____ / 100

Division Facts • ÷ 4's and 5's

5)15	4)12	5)5	5)45	4)0	4)8	5)0	5)35	4)4	5)10
4)16	5)25	4)20	4)36	5)40	4)28	4)24	5)30	4)32	5)20
4)0	5)20	5)5	5)35	4)0	5)30	5)0	4)4	5)25	4)16
4)28	5)10	4)24	4)8	5)10	4)28	5)30	5)15	4)4	5)0
4)8	5)30	5)5	4)0	5)15	4)12	4)16	4)24	5)35	4)4
4)32	5)10	4)16	5)30	5)40	4)28	4)12	5)15	5)0	4)4
5)35	5)0	5)45	4)32	4)0	5)25	4)16	4)12	5)30	5)5
5)20	4)24	5)25	4)4	5)10	4)12	4)8	4)16	5)35	5)30
5)25	5)0	4)28	5)30	5)5	4)12	5)35	5)20	5)40	4)36
4)16	5)5	4)12	5)25	5)45	4)36	5)40	5)15	4)24	5)35

Division Facts • ÷ 5's and 6's

$5\overline{)25}$ $6\overline{)12}$ $5\overline{)45}$ $6\overline{)48}$ $5\overline{)0}$ $6\overline{)6}$ $5\overline{)15}$ $5\overline{)5}$ $6\overline{)30}$ $6\overline{)6}$

$5\overline{)10}$ $6\overline{)18}$ $6\overline{)42}$ $6\overline{)36}$ $6\overline{)30}$ $5\overline{)20}$ $5\overline{)40}$ $6\overline{)24}$ $6\overline{)54}$ $5\overline{)35}$

$6\overline{)42}$ $5\overline{)15}$ $5\overline{)45}$ $6\overline{)24}$ $6\overline{)0}$ $5\overline{)20}$ $5\overline{)40}$ $5\overline{)25}$ $6\overline{)42}$ $6\overline{)30}$

$5\overline{)0}$ $6\overline{)6}$ $5\overline{)20}$ $6\overline{)12}$ $6\overline{)54}$ $6\overline{)0}$ $5\overline{)45}$ $5\overline{)20}$ $6\overline{)36}$ $5\overline{)40}$

$6\overline{)24}$ $6\overline{)12}$ $5\overline{)25}$ $6\overline{)0}$ $5\overline{)5}$ $5\overline{)15}$ $6\overline{)12}$ $6\overline{)0}$ $6\overline{)48}$ $5\overline{)45}$

$5\overline{)25}$ $6\overline{)48}$ $6\overline{)42}$ $5\overline{)0}$ $6\overline{)30}$ $6\overline{)36}$ $6\overline{)18}$ $6\overline{)6}$ $5\overline{)5}$ $5\overline{)15}$

$5\overline{)40}$ $6\overline{)36}$ $6\overline{)12}$ $6\overline{)24}$ $5\overline{)25}$ $6\overline{)48}$ $5\overline{)20}$ $5\overline{)0}$ $6\overline{)18}$ $5\overline{)45}$

$6\overline{)0}$ $5\overline{)20}$ $6\overline{)18}$ $5\overline{)0}$ $6\overline{)6}$ $6\overline{)36}$ $6\overline{)42}$ $5\overline{)35}$ $5\overline{)15}$ $6\overline{)0}$

$6\overline{)36}$ $5\overline{)25}$ $5\overline{)45}$ $6\overline{)24}$ $5\overline{)40}$ $5\overline{)5}$ $5\overline{)0}$ $5\overline{)35}$ $6\overline{)12}$ $5\overline{)20}$

$5\overline{)35}$ $5\overline{)30}$ $6\overline{)36}$ $5\overline{)40}$ $6\overline{)42}$ $5\overline{)15}$ $6\overline{)12}$ $5\overline{)10}$ $6\overline{)48}$ $5\overline{)45}$

Name _____

Division Facts • *÷ 6's and 7's*

6⟌18	7⟌7	6⟌42	7⟌21	6⟌6	7⟌0	6⟌12	7⟌42	7⟌14	6⟌54
7⟌28	6⟌30	7⟌35	6⟌24	7⟌49	6⟌48	6⟌0	7⟌56	7⟌63	6⟌36
7⟌7	6⟌24	7⟌42	6⟌54	7⟌0	6⟌6	7⟌21	6⟌24	6⟌12	7⟌35
6⟌36	7⟌0	7⟌49	6⟌48	7⟌63	7⟌21	6⟌12	7⟌7	6⟌24	7⟌14
7⟌56	7⟌7	6⟌18	6⟌6	7⟌35	6⟌12	7⟌49	7⟌56	6⟌54	7⟌63
6⟌12	7⟌21	6⟌24	7⟌35	6⟌48	6⟌42	7⟌56	7⟌0	6⟌6	6⟌30
7⟌21	7⟌28	6⟌48	6⟌36	7⟌14	7⟌63	6⟌0	7⟌21	6⟌18	6⟌30
6⟌54	6⟌0	7⟌14	6⟌18	6⟌30	6⟌12	7⟌28	7⟌35	6⟌48	7⟌63
7⟌49	7⟌42	6⟌24	6⟌30	7⟌28	6⟌6	7⟌0	7⟌56	7⟌21	6⟌12
7⟌42	6⟌18	7⟌35	6⟌36	6⟌30	7⟌21	6⟌24	6⟌54	7⟌56	7⟌7

Division Facts • ÷ 7's and 8's

$8\overline{)0}$ $7\overline{)35}$ $8\overline{)16}$ $7\overline{)14}$ $8\overline{)64}$ $7\overline{)49}$ $7\overline{)28}$ $8\overline{)40}$ $8\overline{)8}$ $7\overline{)63}$

$8\overline{)24}$ $8\overline{)32}$ $8\overline{)48}$ $7\overline{)0}$ $7\overline{)21}$ $8\overline{)56}$ $7\overline{)7}$ $7\overline{)42}$ $8\overline{)72}$ $7\overline{)56}$

$8\overline{)64}$ $7\overline{)35}$ $8\overline{)0}$ $7\overline{)42}$ $8\overline{)16}$ $7\overline{)0}$ $8\overline{)8}$ $7\overline{)49}$ $8\overline{)48}$ $8\overline{)24}$

$7\overline{)42}$ $8\overline{)32}$ $7\overline{)35}$ $8\overline{)48}$ $7\overline{)49}$ $8\overline{)16}$ $7\overline{)63}$ $8\overline{)64}$ $7\overline{)0}$ $8\overline{)8}$

$7\overline{)28}$ $8\overline{)40}$ $7\overline{)35}$ $8\overline{)24}$ $7\overline{)28}$ $8\overline{)0}$ $7\overline{)7}$ $7\overline{)56}$ $7\overline{)28}$ $8\overline{)64}$

$8\overline{)24}$ $8\overline{)56}$ $7\overline{)14}$ $7\overline{)49}$ $8\overline{)40}$ $8\overline{)8}$ $7\overline{)21}$ $8\overline{)32}$ $7\overline{)35}$ $8\overline{)40}$

$7\overline{)56}$ $8\overline{)24}$ $7\overline{)0}$ $7\overline{)28}$ $8\overline{)48}$ $7\overline{)56}$ $8\overline{)72}$ $8\overline{)56}$ $7\overline{)56}$ $7\overline{)63}$

$8\overline{)72}$ $7\overline{)7}$ $7\overline{)49}$ $8\overline{)32}$ $7\overline{)14}$ $7\overline{)35}$ $8\overline{)64}$ $8\overline{)16}$ $7\overline{)0}$ $8\overline{)24}$

$8\overline{)8}$ $7\overline{)35}$ $8\overline{)48}$ $7\overline{)63}$ $8\overline{)64}$ $7\overline{)7}$ $8\overline{)0}$ $7\overline{)35}$ $8\overline{)48}$ $8\overline{)72}$

$7\overline{)49}$ $8\overline{)0}$ $7\overline{)7}$ $7\overline{)42}$ $8\overline{)56}$ $7\overline{)42}$ $8\overline{)40}$ $8\overline{)56}$ $7\overline{)14}$ $8\overline{)32}$

Name _____   Time _____

Division Facts • ÷ 8's and 9's

$9\overline{)0}$ $8\overline{)8}$ $9\overline{)18}$ $8\overline{)24}$ $9\overline{)63}$ $8\overline{)16}$ $9\overline{)81}$ $8\overline{)48}$ $9\overline{)9}$ $8\overline{)0}$

$8\overline{)32}$ $9\overline{)27}$ $8\overline{)40}$ $9\overline{)36}$ $8\overline{)56}$ $9\overline{)45}$ $8\overline{)64}$ $9\overline{)54}$ $8\overline{)72}$ $9\overline{)72}$

$8\overline{)0}$ $8\overline{)64}$ $9\overline{)18}$ $9\overline{)81}$ $8\overline{)8}$ $8\overline{)32}$ $9\overline{)27}$ $8\overline{)40}$ $9\overline{)9}$ $8\overline{)56}$

$8\overline{)48}$ $9\overline{)18}$ $8\overline{)0}$ $8\overline{)24}$ $9\overline{)36}$ $9\overline{)9}$ $8\overline{)48}$ $9\overline{)63}$ $8\overline{)56}$ $9\overline{)0}$

$8\overline{)56}$ $8\overline{)32}$ $9\overline{)18}$ $9\overline{)72}$ $8\overline{)48}$ $8\overline{)0}$ $9\overline{)18}$ $9\overline{)36}$ $9\overline{)9}$ $8\overline{)16}$

$9\overline{)0}$ $8\overline{)48}$ $8\overline{)72}$ $9\overline{)45}$ $8\overline{)64}$ $9\overline{)18}$ $9\overline{)27}$ $8\overline{)32}$ $9\overline{)81}$ $8\overline{)40}$

$9\overline{)36}$ $9\overline{)81}$ $8\overline{)0}$ $9\overline{)27}$ $8\overline{)16}$ $9\overline{)36}$ $9\overline{)63}$ $8\overline{)48}$ $8\overline{)56}$ $8\overline{)0}$

$9\overline{)81}$ $8\overline{)24}$ $9\overline{)36}$ $8\overline{)8}$ $8\overline{)16}$ $9\overline{)36}$ $9\overline{)18}$ $8\overline{)40}$ $9\overline{)36}$ $8\overline{)32}$

$9\overline{)18}$ $9\overline{)0}$ $8\overline{)8}$ $8\overline{)56}$ $9\overline{)45}$ $8\overline{)48}$ $8\overline{)64}$ $9\overline{)81}$ $9\overline{)9}$ $8\overline{)72}$

$8\overline{)40}$ $9\overline{)27}$ $8\overline{)0}$ $8\overline{)16}$ $9\overline{)27}$ $8\overline{)32}$ $9\overline{)36}$ $8\overline{)40}$ $9\overline{)9}$ $8\overline{)32}$

Division Facts • ÷ 1's, 2's, 3's, and 4's

$1\overline{)1}$	$2\overline{)10}$	$3\overline{)3}$	$4\overline{)24}$	$2\overline{)0}$	$1\overline{)5}$	$2\overline{)16}$	$4\overline{)12}$	$2\overline{)0}$	$3\overline{)15}$
$4\overline{)8}$	$1\overline{)2}$	$4\overline{)16}$	$2\overline{)6}$	$3\overline{)24}$	$2\overline{)2}$	$4\overline{)28}$	$4\overline{)24}$	$3\overline{)9}$	$1\overline{)3}$
$2\overline{)4}$	$1\overline{)6}$	$4\overline{)36}$	$2\overline{)12}$	$3\overline{)9}$	$2\overline{)10}$	$1\overline{)7}$	$3\overline{)15}$	$4\overline{)32}$	$4\overline{)20}$
$4\overline{)0}$	$1\overline{)3}$	$1\overline{)2}$	$4\overline{)16}$	$3\overline{)12}$	$2\overline{)8}$	$2\overline{)8}$	$3\overline{)0}$	$4\overline{)4}$	$3\overline{)21}$
$3\overline{)27}$	$2\overline{)14}$	$4\overline{)24}$	$1\overline{)0}$	$4\overline{)4}$	$2\overline{)14}$	$1\overline{)6}$	$3\overline{)15}$	$2\overline{)18}$	$1\overline{)8}$
$1\overline{)7}$	$1\overline{)9}$	$2\overline{)10}$	$1\overline{)5}$	$3\overline{)12}$	$2\overline{)6}$	$3\overline{)18}$	$4\overline{)20}$	$3\overline{)27}$	$2\overline{)16}$
$4\overline{)4}$	$4\overline{)36}$	$2\overline{)4}$	$3\overline{)9}$	$1\overline{)3}$	$4\overline{)4}$	$4\overline{)36}$	$1\overline{)2}$	$3\overline{)15}$	$1\overline{)1}$
$4\overline{)16}$	$1\overline{)9}$	$4\overline{)32}$	$1\overline{)7}$	$4\overline{)20}$	$2\overline{)14}$	$4\overline{)20}$	$3\overline{)9}$	$2\overline{)16}$	$1\overline{)6}$
$2\overline{)18}$	$3\overline{)18}$	$2\overline{)0}$	$1\overline{)8}$	$2\overline{)12}$	$4\overline{)16}$	$3\overline{)15}$	$2\overline{)8}$	$3\overline{)27}$	$2\overline{)16}$
$3\overline{)21}$	$2\overline{)8}$	$2\overline{)18}$	$3\overline{)24}$	$2\overline{)12}$	$1\overline{)3}$	$4\overline{)4}$	$3\overline{)9}$	$4\overline{)16}$	$4\overline{)36}$

Division Facts • ÷ 5's, 6's, 7's, 8's, and 9's

$5\overline{)0}$ $8\overline{)16}$ $6\overline{)42}$ $5\overline{)25}$ $6\overline{)12}$ $8\overline{)48}$ $9\overline{)0}$ $5\overline{)5}$ $7\overline{)14}$ $6\overline{)0}$

$9\overline{)9}$ $8\overline{)40}$ $7\overline{)0}$ $6\overline{)36}$ $5\overline{)20}$ $6\overline{)54}$ $8\overline{)0}$ $9\overline{)18}$ $8\overline{)64}$ $6\overline{)24}$

$8\overline{)24}$ $6\overline{)0}$ $5\overline{)10}$ $9\overline{)81}$ $5\overline{)30}$ $6\overline{)6}$ $5\overline{)35}$ $9\overline{)54}$ $7\overline{)21}$ $5\overline{)40}$

$7\overline{)28}$ $8\overline{)8}$ $5\overline{)15}$ $8\overline{)32}$ $9\overline{)27}$ $7\overline{)63}$ $6\overline{)30}$ $5\overline{)45}$ $9\overline{)72}$ $7\overline{)42}$

$6\overline{)48}$ $7\overline{)35}$ $6\overline{)18}$ $9\overline{)63}$ $8\overline{)56}$ $9\overline{)18}$ $8\overline{)72}$ $7\overline{)56}$ $9\overline{)45}$ $7\overline{)7}$

$5\overline{)0}$ $6\overline{)12}$ $9\overline{)18}$ $8\overline{)32}$ $6\overline{)30}$ $5\overline{)20}$ $8\overline{)16}$ $8\overline{)0}$ $5\overline{)40}$ $9\overline{)81}$

$5\overline{)35}$ $7\overline{)14}$ $8\overline{)8}$ $6\overline{)36}$ $9\overline{)63}$ $6\overline{)18}$ $6\overline{)6}$ $8\overline{)64}$ $9\overline{)27}$ $6\overline{)0}$

$8\overline{)40}$ $6\overline{)48}$ $9\overline{)36}$ $9\overline{)18}$ $8\overline{)32}$ $6\overline{)30}$ $9\overline{)18}$ $7\overline{)35}$ $7\overline{)7}$ $5\overline{)20}$

$9\overline{)18}$ $5\overline{)25}$ $6\overline{)36}$ $7\overline{)49}$ $9\overline{)72}$ $9\overline{)45}$ $8\overline{)32}$ $5\overline{)10}$ $9\overline{)63}$ $8\overline{)8}$

$7\overline{)42}$ $6\overline{)54}$ $9\overline{)63}$ $6\overline{)0}$ $9\overline{)9}$ $6\overline{)18}$ $5\overline{)20}$ $8\overline{)64}$ $9\overline{)81}$ $5\overline{)25}$

Division Facts • *All Facts*

3⟌18	9⟌63	8⟌32	3⟌21	7⟌35	3⟌3	2⟌14	1⟌4	2⟌12	7⟌56
8⟌56	8⟌72	5⟌20	3⟌3	6⟌12	8⟌24	9⟌54	2⟌2	1⟌5	4⟌36
1⟌7	6⟌24	6⟌30	1⟌9	9⟌72	7⟌49	7⟌21	5⟌5	7⟌21	5⟌25
9⟌63	2⟌4	2⟌18	6⟌48	5⟌20	4⟌8	4⟌32	1⟌6	4⟌16	1⟌1
4⟌4	6⟌36	3⟌9	6⟌54	5⟌35	4⟌20	3⟌24	9⟌81	6⟌42	9⟌27
6⟌0	2⟌6	3⟌18	4⟌12	8⟌16	8⟌64	6⟌42	6⟌18	5⟌20	9⟌81
4⟌28	1⟌7	2⟌8	8⟌48	5⟌45	4⟌0	2⟌10	5⟌15	1⟌4	3⟌27
9⟌54	2⟌8	7⟌49	4⟌36	6⟌36	3⟌15	7⟌42	4⟌12	2⟌6	5⟌40
3⟌15	7⟌49	8⟌8	5⟌40	2⟌14	5⟌45	3⟌15	5⟌25	2⟌4	5⟌10
2⟌6	5⟌45	8⟌72	7⟌56	9⟌36	8⟌40	2⟌16	1⟌3	4⟌24	5⟌30

Name _____

Division Facts • *All Facts*

25 ÷ 5 = _____	40 ÷ 5 = _____	15 ÷ 5 = _____	45 ÷ 5 = _____	40 ÷ 5 = _____
18 ÷ 6 = _____	54 ÷ 6 = _____	12 ÷ 6 = _____	24 ÷ 6 = _____	48 ÷ 6 = _____
0 ÷ 7 = _____	21 ÷ 7 = _____	35 ÷ 7 = _____	49 ÷ 7 = _____	42 ÷ 7 = _____
16 ÷ 8 = _____	16 ÷ 8 = _____	64 ÷ 8 = _____	16 ÷ 8 = _____	40 ÷ 5 = _____
9 ÷ 9 = _____	63 ÷ 9 = _____	27 ÷ 9 = _____	40 ÷ 8 = _____	48 ÷ 6 = _____
35 ÷ 5 = _____	20 ÷ 5 = _____	15 ÷ 5 = _____	15 ÷ 5 = _____	49 ÷ 7 = _____
36 ÷ 6 = _____	30 ÷ 6 = _____	18 ÷ 6 = _____	12 ÷ 6 = _____	45 ÷ 5 = _____
49 ÷ 7 = _____	28 ÷ 7 = _____	63 ÷ 7 = _____	28 ÷ 7 = _____	12 ÷ 6 = _____
40 ÷ 8 = _____	16 ÷ 8 = _____	48 ÷ 8 = _____	72 ÷ 8 = _____	63 ÷ 7 = _____
27 ÷ 9 = _____	72 ÷ 9 = _____	18 ÷ 9 = _____	27 ÷ 9 = _____	72 ÷ 8 = _____
40 ÷ 5 = _____	30 ÷ 5 = _____	0 ÷ 5 = _____	10 ÷ 5 = _____	42 ÷ 7 = _____
48 ÷ 6 = _____	0 ÷ 6 = _____	48 ÷ 6 = _____	42 ÷ 6 = _____	9 ÷ 9 = _____
42 ÷ 7 = _____	7 ÷ 7 = _____	21 ÷ 7 = _____	14 ÷ 7 = _____	5 ÷ 5 = _____
0 ÷ 8 = _____	72 ÷ 8 = _____	32 ÷ 8 = _____	8 ÷ 8 = _____	18 ÷ 6 = _____
81 ÷ 9 = _____	54 ÷ 9 = _____	0 ÷ 9 = _____	9 ÷ 9 = _____	0 ÷ 7 = _____
5 ÷ 5 = _____	45 ÷ 5 = _____	25 ÷ 5 = _____	0 ÷ 5 = _____	64 ÷ 8 = _____
24 ÷ 6 = _____	16 ÷ 2 = _____	36 ÷ 6 = _____	54 ÷ 6 = _____	20 ÷ 5 = _____
56 ÷ 7 = _____	42 ÷ 7 = _____	14 ÷ 7 = _____	7 ÷ 7 = _____	36 ÷ 6 = _____
32 ÷ 8 = _____	16 ÷ 8 = _____	24 ÷ 8 = _____	0 ÷ 8 = _____	42 ÷ 7 = _____
2 ÷ 1 = _____	0 ÷ 9 = _____	18 ÷ 2 = _____	0 ÷ 9 = _____	63 ÷ 7 = _____
45 ÷ 5 = _____	15 ÷ 5 = _____	35 ÷ 5 = _____	10 ÷ 5 = _____	48 ÷ 8 = _____
12 ÷ 6 = _____	6 ÷ 3 = _____	30 ÷ 6 = _____	48 ÷ 6 = _____	18 ÷ 9 = _____
63 ÷ 7 = _____	7 ÷ 1 = _____	21 ÷ 7 = _____	0 ÷ 7 = _____	12 ÷ 4 = _____
72 ÷ 8 = _____	8 ÷ 8 = _____	0 ÷ 8 = _____	16 ÷ 8 = _____	15 ÷ 5 = _____
36 ÷ 9 = _____	45 ÷ 9 = _____	81 ÷ 9 = _____	18 ÷ 9 = _____	18 ÷ 6 = _____

Division Facts • *÷ 1's, 2's, 3's, and 4's*

$1\overline{)3}$	$2\overline{)6}$	$3\overline{)9}$	$4\overline{)0}$	$1\overline{)5}$
$1\overline{)9}$	$2\overline{)18}$	$3\overline{)0}$	$4\overline{)12}$	$2\overline{)2}$
$1\overline{)7}$	$2\overline{)8}$	$3\overline{)21}$	$4\overline{)16}$	$1\overline{)9}$
$1\overline{)1}$	$2\overline{)4}$	$3\overline{)12}$	$4\overline{)20}$	$3\overline{)12}$
$1\overline{)4}$	$2\overline{)12}$	$3\overline{)18}$	$4\overline{)36}$	$2\overline{)16}$
$1\overline{)8}$	$2\overline{)10}$	$3\overline{)3}$	$4\overline{)4}$	$4\overline{)8}$
$1\overline{)6}$	$2\overline{)0}$	$3\overline{)15}$	$4\overline{)24}$	$1\overline{)5}$
$1\overline{)0}$	$2\overline{)2}$	$3\overline{)6}$	$4\overline{)8}$	$2\overline{)16}$
$1\overline{)5}$	$2\overline{)12}$	$3\overline{)27}$	$4\overline{)28}$	$4\overline{)32}$
$1\overline{)2}$	$2\overline{)14}$	$3\overline{)24}$	$4\overline{)16}$	$4\overline{)20}$

Division Facts • ÷ 5's, 6's, 7's, 8's, and 9's

5)15	6)18	7)14	8)8	9)18
5)45	6)6	7)0	8)48	9)63
5)20	6)48	7)42	8)40	9)81
5)10	6)30	7)21	8)72	9)45
5)30	6)12	7)28	8)32	9)72
5)0	6)54	7)35	8)0	9)9
5)40	6)36	7)7	8)64	9)27
5)5	6)24	7)63	8)24	9)36
5)25	6)42	7)49	8)56	9)0
5)35	6)0	7)56	8)16	9)54

Name _____

Division Facts • ÷ 1's, 2's, and 3's

5 ÷ 1 = _____	21 ÷ 3 = _____	5 ÷ 1 = _____	14 ÷ 2 = _____	27 ÷ 3 = _____
18 ÷ 3 = _____	2 ÷ 2 = _____	4 ÷ 2 = _____	24 ÷ 3 = _____	4 ÷ 1 = _____
0 ÷ 2 = _____	10 ÷ 2 = _____	4 ÷ 1 = _____	9 ÷ 3 = _____	18 ÷ 2 = _____
4 ÷ 2 = _____	8 ÷ 1 = _____	3 ÷ 3 = _____	21 ÷ 3 = _____	12 ÷ 2 = _____
9 ÷ 3 = _____	10 ÷ 2 = _____	9 ÷ 3 = _____	6 ÷ 2 = _____	16 ÷ 2 = _____
5 ÷ 1 = _____	12 ÷ 2 = _____	15 ÷ 3 = _____	12 ÷ 3 = _____	8 ÷ 2 = _____
12 ÷ 3 = _____	27 ÷ 3 = _____	18 ÷ 3 = _____	12 ÷ 2 = _____	0 ÷ 2 = _____
16 ÷ 2 = _____	12 ÷ 2 = _____	27 ÷ 3 = _____	27 ÷ 3 = _____	24 ÷ 3 = _____
4 ÷ 2 = _____	16 ÷ 2 = _____	9 ÷ 3 = _____	10 ÷ 2 = _____	1 ÷ 1 = _____
7 ÷ 1 = _____	8 ÷ 2 = _____	18 ÷ 3 = _____	9 ÷ 3 = _____	3 ÷ 1 = _____
0 ÷ 2 = _____	12 ÷ 3 = _____	0 ÷ 1 = _____	21 ÷ 3 = _____	0 ÷ 2 = _____
18 ÷ 2 = _____	6 ÷ 2 = _____	4 ÷ 2 = _____	12 ÷ 2 = _____	18 ÷ 3 = _____
21 ÷ 3 = _____	6 ÷ 3 = _____	21 ÷ 3 = _____	24 ÷ 3 = _____	5 ÷ 1 = _____
10 ÷ 2 = _____	2 ÷ 2 = _____	14 ÷ 2 = _____	2 ÷ 2 = _____	18 ÷ 2 = _____
8 ÷ 2 = _____	10 ÷ 2 = _____	7 ÷ 1 = _____	9 ÷ 1 = _____	0 ÷ 3 = _____
24 ÷ 3 = _____	12 ÷ 2 = _____	2 ÷ 1 = _____	1 ÷ 1 = _____	12 ÷ 3 = _____
6 ÷ 2 = _____	24 ÷ 3 = _____	3 ÷ 3 = _____	12 ÷ 2 = _____	5 ÷ 1 = _____
40 ÷ 5 = _____	18 ÷ 2 = _____	24 ÷ 3 = _____	6 ÷ 1 = _____	6 ÷ 2 = _____
8 ÷ 4 = _____	16 ÷ 2 = _____	6 ÷ 2 = _____	0 ÷ 3 = _____	12 ÷ 2 = _____
9 ÷ 1 = _____	10 ÷ 2 = _____	9 ÷ 3 = _____	10 ÷ 2 = _____	3 ÷ 1 = _____
5 ÷ 1 = _____	4 ÷ 2 = _____	3 ÷ 1 = _____	9 ÷ 3 = _____	6 ÷ 2 = _____
12 ÷ 2 = _____	0 ÷ 1 = _____	3 ÷ 3 = _____	0 ÷ 2 = _____	5 ÷ 1 = _____
3 ÷ 3 = _____	7 ÷ 1 = _____	8 ÷ 1 = _____	1 ÷ 1 = _____	21 ÷ 3 = _____
21 ÷ 3 = _____	18 ÷ 2 = _____	10 ÷ 2 = _____	9 ÷ 3 = _____	15 ÷ 3 = _____
12 ÷ 3 = _____	8 ÷ 2 = _____	21 ÷ 3 = _____	18 ÷ 2 = _____	18 ÷ 2 = _____

24

Division Facts • ÷ *4's, 5's, and 6's*

25 ÷ 5 = ___	20 ÷ 4 = ___	15 ÷ 5 = ___	45 ÷ 5 = ___	40 ÷ 5 = ___
18 ÷ 6 = ___	54 ÷ 6 = ___	0 ÷ 6 = ___	24 ÷ 6 = ___	48 ÷ 6 = ___
10 ÷ 5 = ___	28 ÷ 4 = ___	35 ÷ 5 = ___	40 ÷ 5 = ___	45 ÷ 5 = ___
24 ÷ 4 = ___	0 ÷ 4 = ___	6 ÷ 6 = ___	16 ÷ 4 = ___	36 ÷ 6 = ___
10 ÷ 5 = ___	15 ÷ 5 = ___	12 ÷ 6 = ___	20 ÷ 5 = ___	48 ÷ 6 = ___
35 ÷ 5 = ___	20 ÷ 5 = ___	15 ÷ 5 = ___	45 ÷ 5 = ___	6 ÷ 6 = ___
36 ÷ 6 = ___	30 ÷ 6 = ___	36 ÷ 6 = ___	12 ÷ 6 = ___	0 ÷ 5 = ___
12 ÷ 4 = ___	24 ÷ 4 = ___	10 ÷ 5 = ___	28 ÷ 4 = ___	24 ÷ 6 = ___
20 ÷ 4 = ___	16 ÷ 4 = ___	0 ÷ 6 = ___	24 ÷ 4 = ___	20 ÷ 5 = ___
24 ÷ 6 = ___	0 ÷ 4 = ___	18 ÷ 6 = ___	20 ÷ 4 = ___	36 ÷ 4 = ___
10 ÷ 5 = ___	30 ÷ 5 = ___	0 ÷ 5 = ___	12 ÷ 6 = ___	4 ÷ 4 = ___
48 ÷ 6 = ___	0 ÷ 6 = ___	4 ÷ 4 = ___	42 ÷ 6 = ___	24 ÷ 6 = ___
45 ÷ 5 = ___	5 ÷ 5 = ___	20 ÷ 4 = ___	15 ÷ 5 = ___	5 ÷ 5 = ___
20 ÷ 4 = ___	4 ÷ 4 = ___	36 ÷ 4 = ___	12 ÷ 4 = ___	18 ÷ 6 = ___
8 ÷ 4 = ___	48 ÷ 6 = ___	0 ÷ 6 = ___	16 ÷ 4 = ___	10 ÷ 5 = ___
5 ÷ 5 = ___	10 ÷ 5 = ___	25 ÷ 5 = ___	0 ÷ 5 = ___	4 ÷ 4 = ___
24 ÷ 6 = ___	36 ÷ 6 = ___	36 ÷ 6 = ___	54 ÷ 6 = ___	10 ÷ 5 = ___
15 ÷ 5 = ___	40 ÷ 5 = ___	20 ÷ 5 = ___	15 ÷ 5 = ___	6 ÷ 6 = ___
36 ÷ 6 = ___	16 ÷ 4 = ___	24 ÷ 4 = ___	4 ÷ 4 = ___	42 ÷ 6 = ___
16 ÷ 4 = ___	18 ÷ 6 = ___	6 ÷ 6 = ___	54 ÷ 6 = ___	48 ÷ 6 = ___
45 ÷ 5 = ___	25 ÷ 5 = ___	35 ÷ 5 = ___	45 ÷ 5 = ___	8 ÷ 4 = ___
12 ÷ 6 = ___	6 ÷ 6 = ___	30 ÷ 6 = ___	48 ÷ 6 = ___	24 ÷ 6 = ___
36 ÷ 4 = ___	40 ÷ 4 = ___	16 ÷ 4 = ___	10 ÷ 5 = ___	40 ÷ 5 = ___
36 ÷ 6 = ___	8 ÷ 4 = ___	0 ÷ 4 = ___	16 ÷ 4 = ___	15 ÷ 5 = ___
8 ÷ 4 = ___	18 ÷ 6 = ___	25 ÷ 5 = ___	18 ÷ 6 = ___	28 ÷ 4 = ___

Name _____

Division Facts • ÷ 7's, 8's, and 9's

24 ÷ 8 = ____	56 ÷ 7 = ____	48 ÷ 8 = ____	48 ÷ 8 = ____	40 ÷ 8 = ____
18 ÷ 9 = ____	54 ÷ 9 = ____	0 ÷ 9 = ____	27 ÷ 9 = ____	42 ÷ 7 = ____
0 ÷ 8 = ____	28 ÷ 7 = ____	32 ÷ 8 = ____	40 ÷ 8 = ____	16 ÷ 8 = ____
14 ÷ 7 = ____	0 ÷ 7 = ____	9 ÷ 9 = ____	14 ÷ 7 = ____	9 ÷ 9 = ____
16 ÷ 8 = ____	64 ÷ 8 = ____	63 ÷ 9 = ____	32 ÷ 8 = ____	45 ÷ 9 = ____
35 ÷ 7 = ____	16 ÷ 8 = ____	16 ÷ 8 = ____	8 ÷ 8 = ____	72 ÷ 9 = ____
36 ÷ 9 = ____	81 ÷ 9 = ____	18 ÷ 9 = ____	81 ÷ 9 = ____	0 ÷ 8 = ____
42 ÷ 7 = ____	35 ÷ 7 = ____	64 ÷ 8 = ____	28 ÷ 7 = ____	27 ÷ 9 = ____
49 ÷ 7 = ____	21 ÷ 7 = ____	48 ÷ 8 = ____	0 ÷ 9 = ____	72 ÷ 8 = ____
27 ÷ 9 = ____	0 ÷ 7 = ____	81 ÷ 9 = ____	42 ÷ 7 = ____	35 ÷ 7 = ____
0 ÷ 8 = ____	32 ÷ 8 = ____	64 ÷ 8 = ____	0 ÷ 9 = ____	42 ÷ 7 = ____
45 ÷ 9 = ____	36 ÷ 9 = ____	28 ÷ 7 = ____	18 ÷ 9 = ____	54 ÷ 9 = ____
40 ÷ 8 = ____	24 ÷ 8 = ____	21 ÷ 7 = ____	16 ÷ 8 = ____	8 ÷ 8 = ____
21 ÷ 7 = ____	49 ÷ 7 = ____	49 ÷ 7 = ____	14 ÷ 7 = ____	18 ÷ 9 = ____
7 ÷ 7 = ____	72 ÷ 9 = ____	9 ÷ 9 = ____	54 ÷ 9 = ____	16 ÷ 8 = ____
24 ÷ 8 = ____	56 ÷ 8 = ____	24 ÷ 8 = ____	48 ÷ 8 = ____	7 ÷ 7 = ____
63 ÷ 9 = ____	63 ÷ 9 = ____	32 ÷ 8 = ____	54 ÷ 9 = ____	64 ÷ 8 = ____
7 ÷ 7 = ____	40 ÷ 8 = ____	24 ÷ 8 = ____	8 ÷ 8 = ____	54 ÷ 9 = ____
9 ÷ 9 = ____	56 ÷ 7 = ____	21 ÷ 7 = ____	49 ÷ 7 = ____	14 ÷ 7 = ____
63 ÷ 7 = ____	18 ÷ 9 = ____	18 ÷ 9 = ____	63 ÷ 9 = ____	56 ÷ 8 = ____
48 ÷ 8 = ____	24 ÷ 8 = ____	16 ÷ 8 = ____	56 ÷ 8 = ____	49 ÷ 7 = ____
18 ÷ 9 = ____	9 ÷ 9 = ____	0 ÷ 9 = ____	18 ÷ 9 = ____	32 ÷ 8 = ____
0 ÷ 7 = ____	42 ÷ 7 = ____	14 ÷ 7 = ____	48 ÷ 8 = ____	40 ÷ 8 = ____
14 ÷ 7 = ____	24 ÷ 8 = ____	0 ÷ 7 = ____	14 ÷ 7 = ____	16 ÷ 8 = ____
28 ÷ 7 = ____	72 ÷ 9 = ____	9 ÷ 9 = ____	18 ÷ 9 = ____	21 ÷ 7 = ____

Name _____

Division Facts • *All Facts*

24 ÷ 8 = _____	63 ÷ 9 = _____	48 ÷ 8 = _____	48 ÷ 8 = _____	25 ÷ 5 = _____
18 ÷ 6 = _____	54 ÷ 9 = _____	0 ÷ 6 = _____	24 ÷ 3 = _____	48 ÷ 6 = _____
0 ÷ 2 = _____	28 ÷ 7 = _____	14 ÷ 2 = _____	40 ÷ 5 = _____	18 ÷ 3 = _____
4 ÷ 4 = _____	8 ÷ 1 = _____	9 ÷ 9 = _____	21 ÷ 3 = _____	15 ÷ 3 = _____
9 ÷ 3 = _____	16 ÷ 8 = _____	24 ÷ 8 = _____	40 ÷ 8 = _____	2 ÷ 2 = _____
35 ÷ 5 = _____	32 ÷ 8 = _____	15 ÷ 5 = _____	16 ÷ 8 = _____	72 ÷ 9 = _____
12 ÷ 3 = _____	81 ÷ 9 = _____	18 ÷ 9 = _____	12 ÷ 2 = _____	0 ÷ 5 = _____
42 ÷ 7 = _____	24 ÷ 4 = _____	64 ÷ 8 = _____	0 ÷ 7 = _____	24 ÷ 6 = _____
25 ÷ 5 = _____	8 ÷ 1 = _____	48 ÷ 6 = _____	27 ÷ 9 = _____	72 ÷ 8 = _____
27 ÷ 9 = _____	8 ÷ 2 = _____	18 ÷ 6 = _____	42 ÷ 7 = _____	3 ÷ 1 = _____
40 ÷ 5 = _____	32 ÷ 8 = _____	0 ÷ 1 = _____	21 ÷ 3 = _____	0 ÷ 2 = _____
45 ÷ 9 = _____	36 ÷ 9 = _____	4 ÷ 4 = _____	10 ÷ 2 = _____	54 ÷ 9 = _____
45 ÷ 5 = _____	16 ÷ 8 = _____	35 ÷ 7 = _____	16 ÷ 8 = _____	5 ÷ 1 = _____
10 ÷ 2 = _____	49 ÷ 7 = _____	49 ÷ 7 = _____	14 ÷ 7 = _____	18 ÷ 2 = _____
7 ÷ 7 = _____	10 ÷ 2 = _____	20 ÷ 5 = _____	54 ÷ 9 = _____	16 ÷ 8 = _____
5 ÷ 5 = _____	56 ÷ 8 = _____	32 ÷ 8 = _____	48 ÷ 8 = _____	4 ÷ 4 = _____
16 ÷ 8 = _____	6 ÷ 3 = _____	36 ÷ 9 = _____	6 ÷ 2 = _____	20 ÷ 5 = _____
8 ÷ 2 = _____	42 ÷ 6 = _____	20 ÷ 5 = _____	8 ÷ 8 = _____	36 ÷ 6 = _____
7 ÷ 0 = _____	16 ÷ 2 = _____	24 ÷ 4 = _____	49 ÷ 7 = _____	40 ÷ 8 = _____
9 ÷ 1 = _____	18 ÷ 9 = _____	9 ÷ 3 = _____	63 ÷ 9 = _____	27 ÷ 3 = _____
48 ÷ 8 = _____	45 ÷ 5 = _____	3 ÷ 1 = _____	18 ÷ 9 = _____	49 ÷ 7 = _____
12 ÷ 6 = _____	6 ÷ 6 = _____	30 ÷ 6 = _____	35 ÷ 7 = _____	3 ÷ 1 = _____
3 ÷ 3 = _____	7 ÷ 1 = _____	14 ÷ 7 = _____	36 ÷ 6 = _____	30 ÷ 5 = _____
24 ÷ 6 = _____	8 ÷ 2 = _____	10 ÷ 2 = _____	16 ÷ 4 = _____	15 ÷ 5 = _____
28 ÷ 7 = _____	36 ÷ 6 = _____	6 ÷ 3 = _____	18 ÷ 6 = _____	28 ÷ 4 = _____

Division Award

Congratulations!

has passed
all of the Division Facts

in _____ minutes with _____ accuracy.

_____   _____
Date   Teacher

Division Award

Congratulations!

_____

has passed _____ Division Facts

in _____ minutes with _____ accuracy.

_____   _____
Date   Teacher

Name _____

Math Facts
Division

100															
95															
90															
85															
80															
75															
70															
65															
60															
55															
50															
45															
40															
35															
30															
25															
20															
15															
10															
5															
0															
Date															

Exciting Products **Kids Will** *WANT* to Get Their **Hands On!**

Little Readers

Big Fibs, Fake Fables, & Little White Lies .... REM 1069-1070
Mini Mystery Readers .... REM 178B-178C
Beginning Reader Program .... REM 191B-191C
I Wonder...Series .... REM 174B-174C, 5001B-5001C
Improve Reading With Humor .... REM 184B-184C
Hot Sports Readers .... REM 187B-187C

Flash Cards & CDs

Survival Signs & Symbols Program .... REM 1811
Timed Math Flash Cards (+, -, x, ÷) .... REM 179A-179E
Basic Sight Words Program .... REM 180, 486, 180A
Clocks Flash Cards .... REM 4384
Money Flash Cards .... REM 4459

Activity Books

Reading for Speed & Content (3-Book Set) .... REM 1043
Read & Color Series (10-Book Set) .... REM 1060

For More Information, contact us at 1-800-826-4740 • www.rempub.com

RPPG016